ACKNOWLEDGMENT

Many thanks to the people who have shared their ideas with us so this book could be completed; Carol Rowberrry, Alice Bigelow, Vella Hayes, Doris Rose, Joy Heath, Jill Homer, Betty Moss, Ilene Brown, Karen Willardson, and Phyllis Wright.

An extra special thanks to Sally Rydalch who jumped in to help us with encouragement and enthusiasm. We can never thank our families enough for their love and support.

Revised printing 1991
Reprinted August 1995
Reprinted March 1997

Bright Impressions Inc.
2008 Dimple Dell Road
Sandy, Utah 84094
801-571-9744

INDEX

CHOICE & ACCOUNTABILITY

CARNIVAL OF LIFE

PRIZE
25 POINTS
TICKET

The youth will get more from this activity if the real purpose is kept secret.
This can be a fun, spiritual experience for both youth and leaders.

Activity Introduction:

To present the activity you will need to bring:

1 canning jar with lid, partially filled with bleach. Attach an "ACCOUNTABILITY" sign to the front.
1 small, clear drinking glass with the sign "CHOICES" on the front. Fill the glass half full of water.
Liquid food coloring

We all have the power to choose. This glass represents choices we make. (Hold up the glass.) Maybe we decided to go somewhere we shouldn't. (Drop food coloring in glass.) We might choose to talk in a way that isn't pleasing to our Heavenly Father or our parents. (Use another drop of food coloring. Continue describing different wrong choices we might make and add food coloring after each choice.)

Did you know that we are accountable for all the choices we make? We need to think BEFORE we make choices. But if we find ourselves making the wrong choices, we need to stop and pray for guidance and change the things we have done. (Pour bleach into the glass of water.) Remember, we're accountable for our choices. (Talk for a few minutes until the water becomes clear again.) If we plan and prepare, we will make the right choices and our decisions will be as clean and clear as this water. (Hold up the clear glass of water.)

Handout:

Copy on colored card stock and cut out.

"For it must needs be,
that there is an opposition in all things..."
2 Nephi 2:11

Activity:

Begin this activity in the Relief Society room or the chapel. Lock the doors to the cultural hall until it's time for everyone to enter.

After welcoming everyone, sing "Choose the Right." Dismiss them to go to the cultural hall one row at a time. Give each person five talents upon entering the hall.

During the evening, the people portraying Satan and the missionary will mingle with the youth. Throughout the carnival they will try to get the youth to come to their booths. Satan will tempt them to come to the worldly booths and the missionary will try to get them to come to the spiritual booths.

CHOICE & ACCOUNTABILITY

After the carnival has been progressing for about forty-five minutes, the messengers will come in. They will pick people at random and quietly approach them, touch them on the shoulder, and say, "It's time to go." Then they will be escorted to one of the three judges in another room.

The judges will collect their prize and their talent tickets. The youth will be told that any prizes they have won are earthly possessions and they cannot take them with them. Their talents will then be counted and recorded. If they have earned at least 15 talents they will receive the celestial badge. If they have received between 10 and 14, they will receive the Terrestrial badge. If they have received less than 10 talents, they will receive the Telestial badge. These badges will be pinned to their shoulder and an usher will take them to the chapel where they will be seated in the kingdom they have earned.

You may need to give them a word game and a pencil to keep them occupied and quiet until everyone is escorted in.

When everyone has been seated in the chapel, introduce the guest speaker. After the speaker, pass out the handouts and sing "Know This That Every Soul Is Free." This will be followed by the closing prayer and dismissthem to a room where refreshments will be served.

Preparation:

Assign a pianist and chorister for the music.

Prepare light refreshments for the evening.

Copy talent tickets. Each person should have five at the beginning of the program and you will also have talents to be won at the talent booths.

Copy prize tickets for the worldly booths.

Arrange a prize booth with pretend prizes to be won. (The youth do not actually earn these prizes, even if they think they have.) Such as, camera 400 points, cassette tapes 100 points, etc. Assign someone to stay at the prize table throughout the evening to entice them to try to get more points.

Invite a return missionary or an adult to play the part of a missionary. They should be dressed in a plain dark suit with a name badge. His task will be to mingle with the youth during the evening and encourage them to spend time at the spiritual booths.

Invite another adult to play the part of Satan. He will wear flashy, bright colored clothing. His task will be to mingle with the youth during the evening and attempt to influence them to use their time to win prizes at the worldly booths instead of talents at the spiritual booths.

Invite twelve other people to help. Six people to act as messengers, three people as judges, and three people as ushers.

Ask someone to make up a word game to do with choices and accountability. The youth can play this game while waiting for everyone to enter the chapel.

Separate the chapel into three sections indicating the three degrees of glory. The ushers will bring them to the place they have earned.

Assign a speaker to explain about the three degrees of glory. Some references are: Telestial, D&C 76:81:89, Terrestrial, D&C 88: 21-24, D&C 76: 71-80,97, and Celestial, D&C 76:50-70, 92, D&C 131: 1-4, 1 Corinthians 15:40. The speaker should speak about the evening's activity and how it relates to real life.

In a separate room, decorate a long table in white. The judges will sit here as the youth are brought in.

Decorate nine booths: four worldly booths, four spiritual booths, and a prize booth. You should have at least one person to help at each booth. The booths should be decorated with signs, balloons, lights, or anything that will lure the youth. The youth may visit each booth as many times as they desire or time allows.

Supply each of the worldly booths with small candies, cupcakes, or cookies to be earned along with the prizes.

Talent Tickets

Prize Tickets

PRIZE 25 POINTS TICKET	PRIZE 25 POINTS TICKET	PRIZE 25 POINTS TICKET

Worldly Booths

Basketball Throw

The cost for participating at this booth is 1 talent or 50 points. Each player will get three foul shots.

Prize tickets	0 baskets	25 points	
	1 basket	50 points	*If they get at least 2 out of 3 foul shots they receive a treat.*
	2 baskets	75 points	
	3 baskets	100 points	

CHOICE & ACCOUNTABILITY

Golf Booth

The cost for participating at this booth is 1 talent or 50 points. Each player will putt three times.

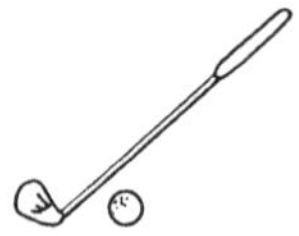

Prize tickets		
	0 putts	25 points
	1 putt	50 points
	2 putts	75 points
	3 putts	100 points

If they get at least 2 out of 3 putts they receive a treat.

Ring Toss

The cost for participating at this booth is 1 talent or 50 points. Each player gets three tosses at a group of plastic soft drink bottles.

Prize tickets		
	0 rings	25 points
	1 ring	50 points
	2 rings	75 points
	3 rings	100 points

If they get at least 2 out of 3 tosses they receive a treat.

Jump Rope

The cost for participating at this booth is 1 talent or 50 points. Each player will get the chance to jump continuously for 100 jumps.

Prize tickets		
	25 jumps	25 points
	50 jumps	50 points
	75 jumps	75 points
	100 jumps	100 points

If they get at least 50 points they receive a treat.

Spiritual Booths

The admission for all spiritual booths is 1 talent. When the youth leave the booth they will receive their original talent back plus the talents they win.

Name That Hymn

The pianist will play three notes of a church hymn. If the youth can identify the song they write it on their paper and turn it in for scoring. If they can't guess the song on three notes, she will play five notes and then seven notes. Change songs frequently.

Scoring		
	7 notes	1 talent
	5 notes	2 talents
	3 notes	3 talents

Name The Prophets

On a bulletin board, place eight pictures of Latter-day prophets with a number by each one. The youth will write down the numbers and the names of each prophet they can identify. Time limit 1 1/2 minutes.

Scoring		
	1 to 2 identified	1 talent
	3 to 5 identified	2 talents
	6 to 8 identified	3 talents

Number The Articles of Faith

Write the 13 Articles of Faith on a poster board. Mix them up and assign a letter from A to M to each one. The youth will write down 13 numbers and write the letter of each Article of Faith by it. For example if the 1st Article of Faith had the letter M in front of it, they would write 1-M. Time limit 3 minutes.

Scoring	1 to 4 correct	1 talent
	5 to 9 correct	2 talents
	9 to 13 correct	3 talents

Name The Books of The Old Testament

On a black board, randomly list the names of six New Testament books, six Old Testament books, and six books of the Book of Mormon. Number them from 1 to 18. Give each player 1 minute to write down the correct numbers of the 6 books in the Old Testament.

Scoring	1 to 2 correct	1 talent
	3 to 4 correct	2 talents
	5 to 6 correct	3 talents

Badges

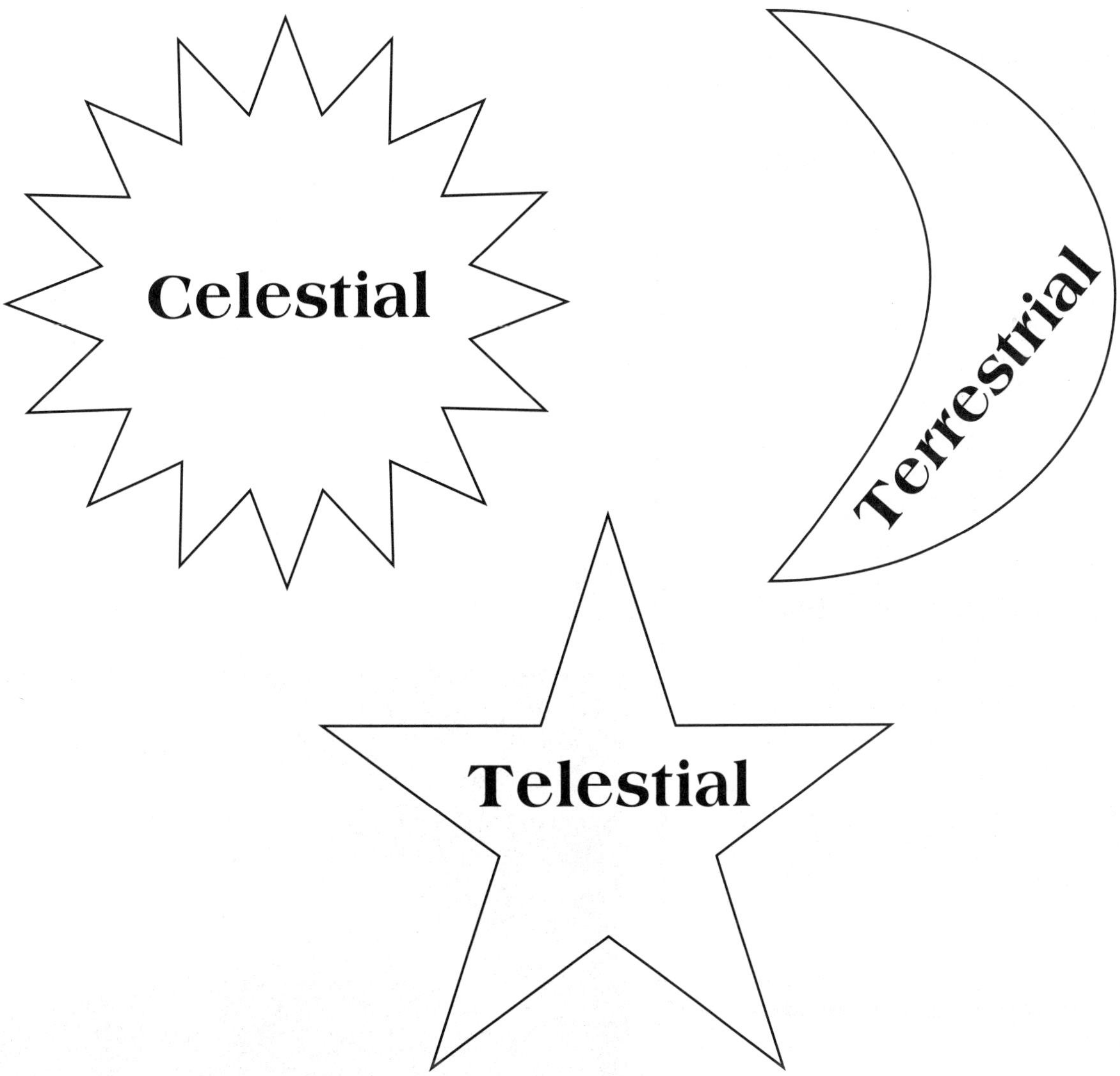

THIS IS YOUR LIFE, BISHOP!

We often refer to Stake leaders or General Authorities when we talk about church leaders.
The Bishop, as our ward father, plays a primary role as our church leader.

Activity Introduction:

To present the activity you will need to bring:

Pair of man's dress shoe with laces

(Hold up one shoe and shoe lace. Lace it as you're speaking.) The ward is a little like this dress shoe. The ward could be the shoelace and the eyelets represent the positions we hold or the classes we're in. (Lace shoe and tie in a bow.) The Bishop is the knot in the bow that ties us all together. (Pass out the picture of the Bishop in the shoe.)

INVITATION:

Fill in the information and copy on heavy paper.

The Bishop is the knot in the bow that ties us all together.

Join us in honoring the Bishop!

There was an old Bishop who lived in a shoe.
He had so many ward members he didn't know what to do.

He led them and blessed them and helped them with ease.
They all lived together as nice as you please.

As our own ward father he keeps us together,
In a nice cozy bow, through all kinds of weather.

Date:

Time:

Place:

Handout:

Copy on colored card stock and cut out.

Bishop, you're the GREATEST!

Activity:

Present the activity, "This is your life, Bishop!" with enthusiasm. The story could go something like this: A long time ago in the city of_______________, a baby boy was born weighing ________. (Show the Bishop's baby picture and continue the story using experiences in his life from childhood to adulthood.) Yes, this is your life, Bishop! *Everyone stands and cheer. When he comes forward, shake his hand and present him with a boutonniere.* You have been important to many people, Bishop. Do you remember when . . . (for example; a sister was crying in the hall because she couldn't get control of her class and you came and offered comfort? Well, Sister _______ remembers! *The sister enters and greets the Bishop.* Then there is another lady who . . . Continue describing three or four people with whom he has had a special experiences.

Preparation:

Assign someone to meet with the bishop's wife to coordinate this activity so he will be surprised. Get a life story about him that only a family member would know. You need to know things like where he was born, childhood experiences, spiritual experiences, etc. It would make the evening more interesting if there were pictures to go along with the story.

Ask someone with a flair for theatrics to present this story.

Invite three or four people that knew the bishop in earlier months or years to be on the program. During the presentation tell about a special incident that happened between them and the bishop.

Find out what his favorite dessert is and present it to him in a special way. This could be a glass pie plate engraved with his name and filled with a pie, or his favorite cake with a note signed by everyone.

Use the opaque projector from the library to display the pictures while telling his life story.

Buy a boutonniere for the bishop.

THE FESTIVAL OF FOREIGN FOLKS

It's important that we learn about people living in other countries. They have so many things to offer: good food, entertainment, different lifestyles, etc.

Activity Introduction:

To present the activity you will need to bring:

10 different rocks in various sizes, shapes, and kinds

Lay the rocks in a row. Look at these rocks. Notice how differently they're shaped. Observe the different colors. These rocks could be likened to people in other lands. Just like these rocks, you can only learn so much about them by just looking. But if you pick them up and study them you discover the different qualities. You can also discover the different qualities in people from other lands by getting close to them and learning more about them. Let's look closer at all people, no matter what nationality, so we can gain better understanding and appreciation for each other.

Invitation:

Make a German Chocolate cake and cut a piece for each person.
Fill in the information and copy the invitation.
Glue the invitation on a toothpick and stand it upright in a piece of cake just before you serve it.

They call America, "The Melting Pot".
Because people of other lands come to live.
Let's learn more about these people,
And all the things they have to give?

Date:
Time:
Place:

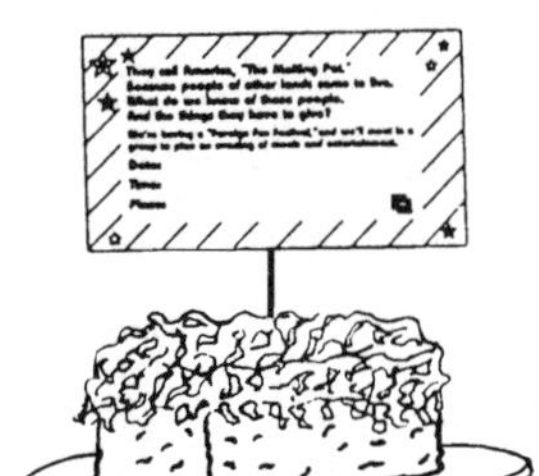

Activity:

Welcome all the people that are representing the different lands. Turn the time over to the guest speaker. After the speech, continue the evening with a buffet style dinner.

After the meal, each group will do their presentation from the land of their choice. End the evening by giving each girl a recipe book.

Preparation:

Invite someone from a different land or someone who has visited a different land to give a short talk about the people, food, dances,and customs.

Assign the girls to work in small groups of four to six. Let them decide which country they want to represent. If possible, let them wear an article of clothing from that land. After deciding on the food they're going to bring, they can plan a short presentation about the food, customs, and people, or a song or dance to present. (Make sure each group brings a different part of the meal so you have main dishes, salads, drinks, and desserts to serve.) You might also suggest they bring signs, decorations, etc. to put by their food item on the buffet table.

Decorate the room with items from different lands.

Collect the recipes used from each group. Copy and put together a cookbook.

Cookbook Cover

Food from the FESTIVAL of FOREIGN FOLKS

THE BEAR ESSENTIALS

Most young women like teddy bears. Let's connect something they enjoy, like teddy bears, to something we're teaching, like divine nature. We'll have a "Very Bear-able Day."

Activity Introduction:

To present the activity you will need to bring:

Bear tracks cut from dark brown or black paper
Tape to attach bear tracks to the wall or floor
A large furry teddy bear
Invitations in a large bowl

The Sunday before the activity, place the bear tracks on the floor and wall of your meeting room, to look as though a bear has walked through. End the tracks in the room where everyone meets. Place a table at the end of the trail. Sit the large teddy bear holding the bowl of very "bearable" invitations on the table. Pass the invitations out. Remind each girl to bring a bear with them to the activity.

Invitations:

Fill in the information needed and copy the invitation.

Do you want to have
A "beary" nice day?
One that's nice
In every way?
Well, live each day
And do your part.
You'll love life,
With all your heart.

Date:

Time:

Place:

Bring your favorite teddy bear.

Activity:

Meet together for an evening of very "bearable" fun. Give each girl a bear name tag as they come in. Spread quilts on the floor. Encourage the girls to take their teddy bears and sit on the quilts and visit until everyone arrives.

After the greeting and prayer, divide into five groups. Each group will go to their assigned "Bear" workshop. Rotate classes every ten minutes so girls can attend them all. After the workshops, meet together again to visit, serve refreshments, and have closing prayer.

Preparation:

Invite five people to give a 10 minute workshop on the subjects below. Each workshop will be given five times. This may need to be adjusted, depending on the size of your group.

Make a large sign for each class. Hang the sign above the classroom door.

Thou Shalt Not "Bear" False witness (Honesty)

"Bear" All Things, Believeth All Things (Faith)

Be Willing To "Bear" Each Other's Burdens (Friendship)

Be Ye Clean That "Bear" The Vessel of The Lord (Chastity)

Find "Buried" Treasures (Scriptures)

Decorate with paw prints and bears. Turn the entire area into a den of "Bear Essentials".

Bring old quilts or blankets to sit on while visiting and eating refreshments.

Make refreshments. (Decorated gingerbread bears would be fun.)

Bear Tag Pattern

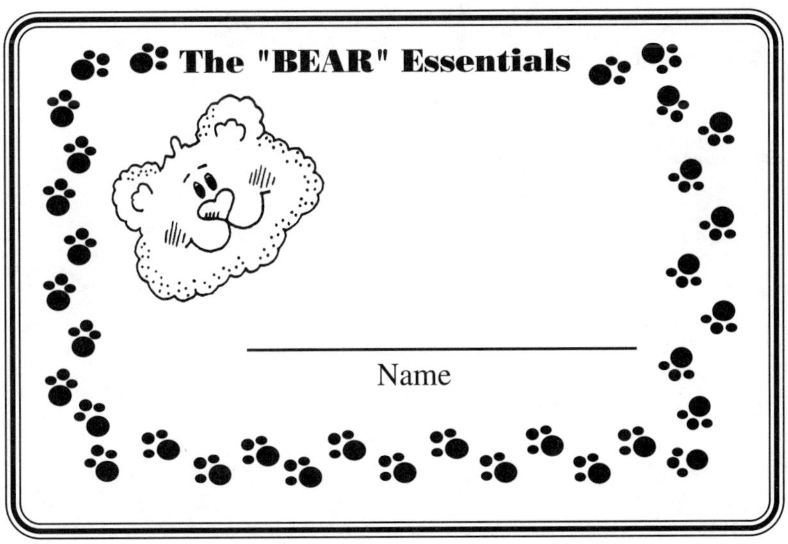

OUR PRICELESS FAITH

Here's a chance to show the girls, through the beauty of nature, how important faith is. We can do this by being away from everything and sharing testimonies.

Activity Introduction:

To present the activity you will need to bring:

A large rock

A small brown paper bag.

Show both articles. Some of us have faith the same size as other people's testimonies, but all testimonies don't consist of the same thing. Show rock. We have to do a lot of hard work to obtain a testimony as hard as a rock." We pray, read scriptures, attend our meetings, etc. Blow up the bag, holding the opening tight so it stays inflated. Often we say we have a testimony because our friend or our teacher or someone in our family has a testimony. We are borrowing theirs, because we do not have one of our own. Our testimony is very light. Hit the bag with the other hand, breaking it. Hold it up. If we are borrowing someone else's testimony, let's work to gain our own. We need to work hard to help our faith grow stronger so our testimonies will be "hard as a rock". Show rock again.

Handout:

Bring a small potted plant for each girl. Copy the verse on colored card stock and cut out. Glue a toothpick to the back of the handout and insert it in the soil of the plant. Give each girl a plant after the activity.

I hope you will excuse me if the tears fall,
but sometimes I like to water my testimony...
it helps it grow.

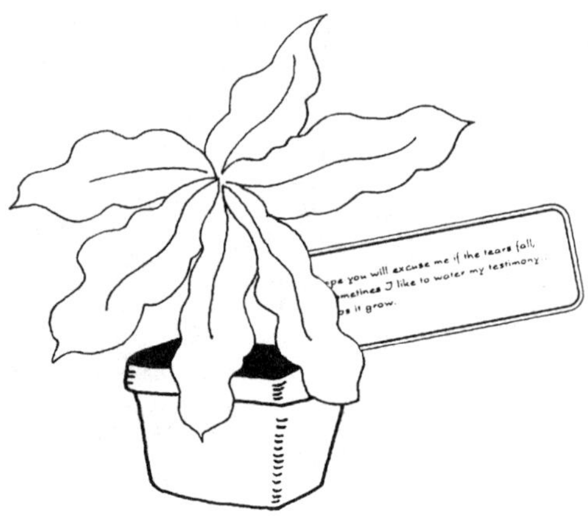

Activity:

Pick up each girl or meet as a group long before sunrise. Be sure everyone has a flashlight. After opening prayer, drive to a secluded area that permits hiking.

As you meet together for instructions let them know you are there to enjoy the beauties of nature and to have a few hours of leisurely time. Gather all their watches so they aren't concerned about the time. Give each girl and leader a "breakfast in a bag" to be eaten later.

Hike together for 10 to 15 minutes, ending in an open area. (Hopefully, just before sunrise.)

Pass out the brown bags with FAITH written on it. Give the girls 10 minutes to put an article of nature in the bag that starts with each letter of the word FAITH.
Give them an additional 10 to 15 minutes to go off to look at nature and meditate.

Call everyone together and turn a few minutes over to the priesthood leader for his talk. End with a short testimony meeting. Be sure that each girl that has a desire, has time to bear her testimony. After the meeting, enjoy your "breakfast in a bag."

Hike back to the cars. Let each girl know how special she is and how important her faith and testimony is. Give each girl a potted plant as you take them home.

Preparation:

Contact the parents ahead of time and let them know when you're meeting or picking up the girls. Ask that each girl brings along a flashlight.

Make a "breakfast in a bag" for each person consisting of something like a carton of milk, a slice of cheese, a large muffin and an apple.

Ask a priesthood leader to attend with you and to talk to the girls about faith and the world around us.

Write the word FAITH on the front of a small brown bag for each girl.

? MYSTERY NIGHT ?

Friendship is something we earn. It's not a gift.
Help the girls realize that friendship is a very special relationship.

Activity Introduction:

To present the activity you will need to bring:

The invitations in a large box wrapped with plain paper and question marks drawn all over it.

(Display the box, but don't talk about it. After the box has received enough attention, pick it up and comment on it.) Everyone loves a mystery. I bet you're wondering what is in this box. Who would like to open it? (After the the box is opened, pass out the invitations.) I want you to think about this box. What do you think these question marks stand for? I hope you spend a lot of time guessing. But you won't know until you come to our Mystery Night and see.

Invitation:

Fill in the information needed and copy.

Refreshments:

Vinegar Pie

2 eggs	2 Tbls. butter
1/2 cup milk	2 cups boiling water
1 1/2 cups sugar	2 1/2 Tbls. vinegar
1/2 tsp salt	
4 Tbls. corn starch	1 cooked pie shell

Beat eggs and add milk. Add dry ingredients and butter. Add boiling water and vinegar. Beat together with a wire whip. Cook until thick. Pour into a cooked pie shell. Cool and top with whipped cream. This recipe is thought to have originated with the pioneers.

Activity:

Give the girls the mystery quiz and five minutes to fill it in. If they don't know the answer to number 18 they can fill it in during the skits whenever they think they know the answer. Present the three skits. After the skits, instruct them to fold their papers and put them in the box. When the skits are over, open the box and read as many answers that time permits until the word "friendship" is found.

Instruct the girls to place their chairs in a large circle. Starting with one girl, ask each girl to say something nice about the girl on her left moving around the circle. The girl speaking takes her right hand, crosses over and clasps the girl's left hand. This girl will then say something nice about the girl on her left and take the other girl's left hand with her right hand. This will continue until the circle is complete.

After playing the circle game, pass out a piece of the Mystery Pie to each girl. After they've eaten, indicate that Friendship is like the mystery ingredient in the pie. That ingredient is vinegar. Like friendship it can be tart and bitter. But mix it with the right ingredients, sugar and butter, or love and care mixed with friendship, it can become something very desirable.

Preparation:

KEEP ALL PREPARATIONS A SECRET.

Assign six adults to assist with the skits. Without the girl's knowledge, find out three different incidents when the girls showed their friendship to each other and act them out in a skit.

Make a copy of the Five Minute Mystery Quiz for each girl. Bring pencils to fill in the quiz and a box to put them in.

Five Minute Mystery Quiz

1. Write your first and middle name.
2. Write the name of the person sitting to the right of you.
3. Where were you born?
4. Where was the person to the left of you born?
5. Shout out your full name.
6. When is your birthday?
7. When is your teacher's birthday?
8. Who do you know the best, the person sitting to the right or to the left of you?
9. When is that person's birthday?
10. Write your mothers maiden name.
11. What is the color of your father's eyes?
12. Ask one of your neighbors to count to ten aloud backwards.
13. Write down the name of the person you talk to most on the phone.
14. Clap you hands over your head three times.
15. What color is the person three chairs to your left wearing?
16. Talk to someone in the group that you haven't talked to for a while.
17. Who was the last person who did something nice for you?
18. The mystery word is ____________________. (If you don't know the mystery word, watch the skits and as soon as you do know the answer, write it in.)

SECRET GRANDMOTHER

The "generation gap" gets wider when we feel so comfortable in our own age group, that we don't put forth the effort needed to find out how many things we all have in common, no matter what our age. Many new friends will be made, if the girls put a generous amount of effort into this activity.

Activity Introduction:

To present the activity you will need to bring:

1 tall clean glass
6 ounces of vinegar
1 Tbls. baking soda
A large dish or pan to catch the overflow

(Display the vinegar.) In your presentation, relate the vinegar to people, especially grandmothers. (Show the baking soda.) Compare it to the friendship that can be felt from the girls. This is you (vinegar) and if we take you and your friendship (baking soda) and add it to the grandmothers, (put baking soda into vinegar) it will make their life "bubble" with joy.

Handout:

Purchase a small potted plant for each grandmother. Copy the card with the verse and put it in the plant. Give a potted plant to each grandmother.

Friendship

Once in a while a friend is found,
who's a friend right from the start,

Once in a while a friendship's made,
that really warms the heart.

Once in a while a friendship's found,
that may last a lifetime through.

It really does happen, just once in a while...
It happened to me and you!

Activity:

Choose secret grandmothers for the girls from your ward, neighborhood, or a rest home. Enjoy several months of the girls performing secret services for their grandmothers, visiting and just getting to know each other better. At the end of that time, the girls will invite their grandmothers to a "Secret Grandmother Luncheon."

As part of the program, the girls can take a few minutes to tell a little about their chosen grandmothers. Bring each grandmother to the front, introduce and tell about her, and present her with a potted plant.

Preparation:

Each girl adopts a secret grandmother for a several month period. They can do acts of kindness for their grandmothers separately, in pairs, or in groups. Below are a few examples of things that the girls can do for their secret grandmothers.

1. *Go to a friend or neighbor of your secret grandmother and learn something about her : such as where she was born, her birth date, her favorite animal, her favorite food, etc.*
2. *Make a dessert (cookies, cake, or brownies) and deliver the treat to her door without her seeing you.*
3. *Drop off a small gift for her on her birthday or another special day.*
4. *Perform a service without her knowing your identity, such as shovel a walk, weed a flower bed, etc.*
5. *Send a card on special occasions.*
6. *On Family Night, drop off a note or treat at her door.*

Let the girls help plan a "Secret Grandmother Luncheon" at the end of their activity. The girls will help plan, prepare, and serve a light lunch. At the luncheon they each will introduce and tell a little bit about their chosen grandmother.

*Alternative plan: If you are short on grandmothers, grandfathers, aunts, or uncles could be adopted instead.

PIG PARTY

Often the youth have been told to improve their manners.
This combined activity will help teach them about manners in a backwaards, humorous way.

Activity Introduction:

To present the activity you will need to:

Ask a couple of girls come in wearing pink pig snouts.

Give them a few moments to snort and carry on like pigs for a minute before leaving. After the demonstration make a few comments on how people often act like pigs. You should have everyone's attention by now, so the invitations can be passed out.

Invitation:

Fill in the information needed and copy on pink card stock. Cut around the outline of the pig.

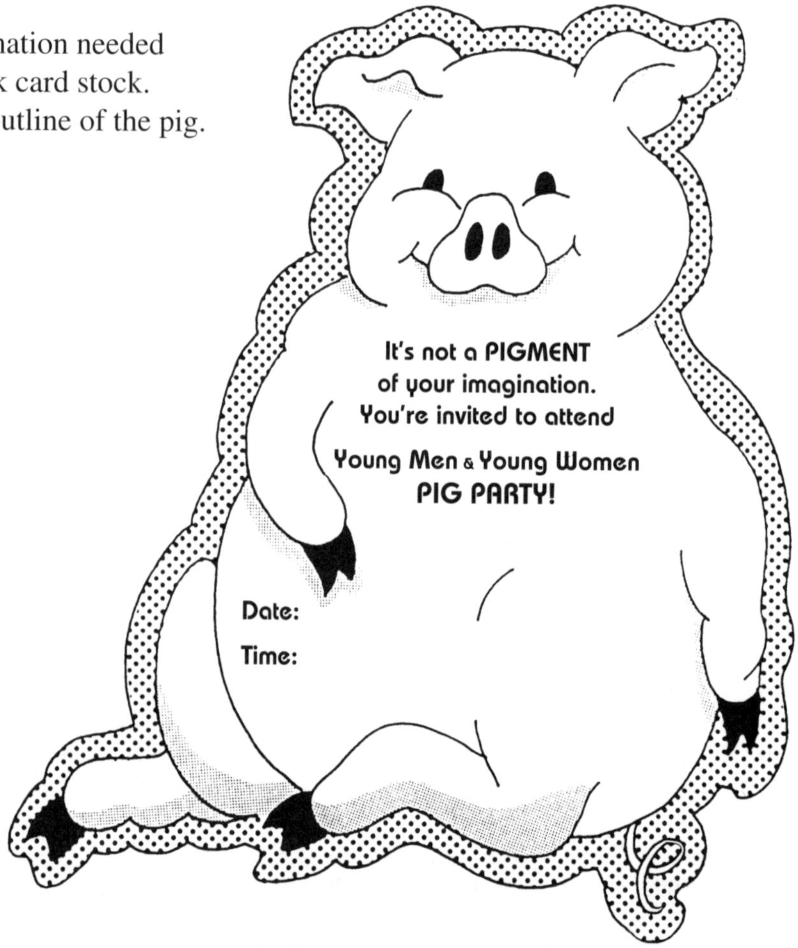

Napkin Ring

Copy and glue one end to the other, forming a ring. Insert napkin through the opening.

Handout:

Copy on pink paper using words to the song, "Swinging On a Star" and pass out during the activity after the skit.

Would you like to swing on a star?
Carry moonbeans home in a jar?
And be better off than you are?
Or would you rather be a pig?

A pig is an animal with dirt on his face.
His shoes are a terrible disgrace.
He's got no manners when he eats his food.
He's fat and lazy and extremely rude.
But if you don't care a feather or a fig.
You may grow up to be a pig!

Activity:

Center everything you do around pigs, for your "Pig Evening."

Pigmania Game Start the activity with a game called Pigmania. Draw pictures of pigs doing various things. The youth will look at each picture and try to guess what it is. Some examples: A pig wearing a sombrero—Pig Latin, A shelf of pig stories—Pig Tales, A pig sitting in a pile of trash— Pig of the Litter, etc.

Pig Out On Pighetti & Meatballs The main part of the activity centers around the dinner. After serving the meal, the youth and leaders put on their pig snouts. Tie their hands to the person next to them and let them try to eat their spaghetti dinner. It's very messy, but lots of fun!

Piggy Playhouse Presents After dinner the Pork Chop Players present their skit. **Swingin' Singin' Swine.**

End the evening with a ridiculous sing-a-long. Change the words to a few songs such as, "Pig O' My Heart" or "Swine On Harvest Moon." Find a song that you can change the words to use "pig" or "swine".

Preparation:

Make a pig snout for each person out of pink egg cartons and string.

Plan and prepare a spaghetti dinner. Lay plastic under the table to make cleanup easier.

Choose two girls to be the Pork Chop Players and perform a skit on manners. They will present a skit such as, "To Grunt Or Not To Grunt." This skit features two pigs; Sophisticated Swine and Sloppy Sow. It's accomplished behind a sheet where one girl stands behind and shows her face through the sheet The other girl sits in front and only shows her arms and hands. To the audience, this looks like only one girl. The girl that can't see, feeds the girl that can, and generally makes a mess. This is very sloppy, but very amusing!

Decorate with pink helium balloons. Draw pig faces on each balloon.

Make napkin rings and insert napkins.

Copy a handout for everyone.

FAVORABLE FAMILY FUN

Our families are very important and each of our families are unique.
This ward family get-together is an entertaining way to show how unusual and fun each family is.

Activity Introduction:

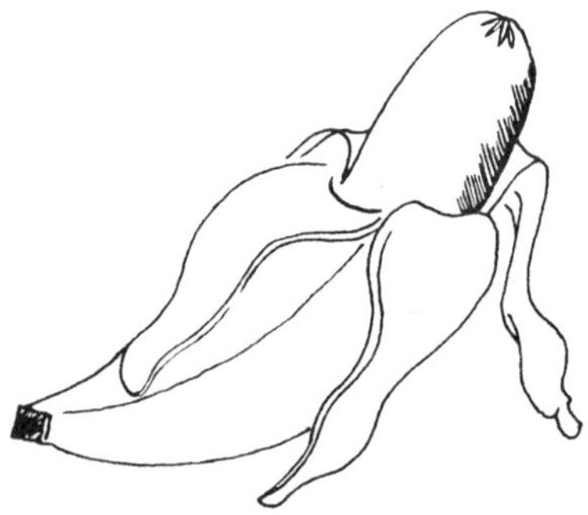

To present the activity you will need to bring:
A bunch of bananas
A hot dog
(Before the meeting, carefully peel one banana from the bottom up, just far enough to scoop the banana out without tearing the peel. Slide the hot dog into the banana peel and tape the bottom end closed with clear tape. Place the bananas in a bowl, with the hotdog-banana toward the middle, so it isn't noticed. Cover with a dish towel.
Uncover the bananas when it's time for the presentation.)

Remind them that all of us grouped together are a little like this bunch of bananas. To the outside world we may all look alike, (Peel a real banana first, then the banana-hot dog exposing the hot dog.) but we're not always what we seem. Some of us have talents hidden inside, like this banana. Pass out the invitations and invite them to a "Favorable Family Fun Night."

Activity:

Start the evening with prayer and the song, "Families Can be Together Forever". Proceed with the show.

Preparation:

Tell all the girls about the big family event and let them know that you would like each of the girls and their families to be represented. If the girl's family can not participate, make sure they are included in another group.

Assign someone to be in charge of the family sign up sheet. Make a program from this list of people contributing their talents.

Assign someone with a entertaining personality to be the master of ceremonies.

Invitation:

Fill in the information, copy, and deliver.

FAVORABLE FAMILY FUN

Our family may look to you, demure.
But, you need to know us too.
When you get us all together,
It's almost like a zoo!

Please bring your family and join us,
With a musical number or a skit.
It doesn't matter what you do.
I know it will really fit!

Date: __________ **Time:** __________ **Place:** __________

Family Name ____________________

Tell us what you'll be doing for your three minute family presentation.

Return paper to ________________ by __________

Leader's name *Date*

YOU ARE THUMB-BODY SPECIAL

This is a good time to learn that we are each unique people with our own individual interesting stories.

Activity Introduction:

To present the activity you will need to bring:

Invite someone to come dressed in clothing from another era

Ask them to tell a short story about an incident that happened in one of their ancestor's life.

For instance, if someone is telling a story about a family member that happened 100 years ago, the young lady can wear a long dress and a bonnet as she describes the sidewalks made of board and how her husband came courting in a horse and buggy, etc. She could end by letting them know that she has come out of the past to tell her story. Her life has helped pave a way for special people like them.

Pass out the "Thum-body Special" form. Instruct them to complete the form by a certain date and return it to their teacher.

Activity:

The Young Women enter and sit on chairs arranged in a large circle. Each girl and leader takes a turn telling her story about her ancestor. (If you have a large group you may want to choose just a few stories to be told.) Half way through the stories, sing a pioneer song and return to the stories.

As the stories are told it may become evident that some of these ancestors lived at the same period and may have known each other and struggled together. Whether your ancestor was a pioneer, convert, immigrant, or a person just trying to promote good in this life, each one left a heritage of strength.

Preparation:

Each leader will be in charge of collecting the "Thumb-Body Special" forms from her group.

Plan ahead if you want to serve refreshments. Serving something from a pioneer cookbook would be fun.

Handout:
Copy and give one to each girl to fill out.

Thumb-Body Special

You are "Thumb-body" special,
Because you are one of a kind.
You're the product of "thumb special" people.
Tell us about them, if you don't mind.

Look at the people way back in the past.
And find "Thumb-body" special like you.
Where they came from, ways they were tested,
And how they were found to be true.

I ________________________ am writing about my
Young women's name

____________________ who is ____________________.
Relationship *Name of ancestor*

Please relate an interesting experience on a separate sheet of paper and attach.

My Ancestors are "Thumb-Body" special to me.

Name of ancestor	*Name of ancestor*	*Name of ancestor*	*Name of ancestor*
Relationship to you	*Relationship to you*	*Relationship to you*	*Relationship to you*
Name of ancestor	*Name of ancestor*	*Name of ancestor*	*Name of ancestor*
Relationship to you	*Relationship to you*	*Relationship to you*	*Relationship to you*

Fill in the information about eight of your different ancestors. Make a thumb print for each person with a stamp pad and draw the face and features.

Please return this completed form to ______________ by ____.
Leader's name *Date*

DARE TO BE SQUARE!

Peer pressure is hard to deal with at this age.
This activity encourages the youth to do what is right, no matter what people may say.

Activity Introduction:

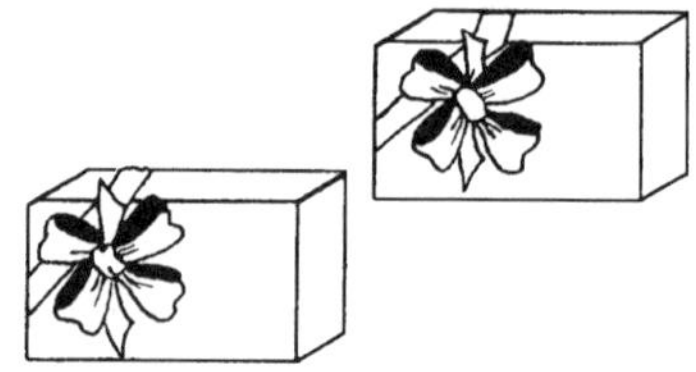

To present the activity you will need to bring:

1 attractively decorated box with filled with cookies for everyone

1 attractively decorated box filled with dirt

(Ahead of time, ask two girls to volunteer without the rest of the group knowing. These two are the only girls that will know what the boxes contain.) Show the two boxes and ask for volunteers to look in a box and describe what they see. (Each of your volunteers look in a box and describes delicious looking cookies.) After the descriptions, ask the group to choose, from the description only, which cookies they would like to eat. Open the boxes and let them see what is in the box they have chosen. Remind them Satan often disguises evil things in attractive packages. Sometimes others try to convince us that something is good when they haven't shown us all the facts.

Invitation:

Fill in information and copy.

DARE TO BE SQUARE NIGHT!

Do you "dare to be square," When you feel all alone?
If you're put to the test, do you sit down and moan?

Well, don't worry, don't fret, you're in for a surprise!
There are more who feel like you— at least those who are wise.

All they need is a leader, someone who looks just like you.
Who will stand up for what they believe, exactly like you do!

Date:

Time:

Place:

Come and join us!

Activity:

Start the activity by reading the poem from the front of the invitation. Follow this with the musical number. The remainder of the time will be spent playing "Dare to be Square Games." If you have too many people in your group, split them up. Each game is for about fourteen people. Serve refreshments after the games.

Preparation:

Get a group to sing the following words to the tune of, "I've Been Working on the Railroad." Alternate song, "It's Hip to be Square" by Huey Lewis.

I've been making life's choices, each and every day.
I've been making life's choices, as the time is passing away.

Can't ya hear the devil calling? Rise up so early if you dare.
Can't ya hear the devil saying? You don't want to be square.

Bring the items needed for each game.

Prepare any dessert shaped like a square for the refreshments.

Dare to be Square Games

Can You Tell Who The Squares Really Are? Leader information: You will need six people to do the coaching (three for the positive side and three for the negative side), the leader to give instructions, and two "ministering angels" for each side. These people will be on the sidelines and no one should know at first that they are part of the game. They are the only ones who know that there is a positive and negative side to the game and what the outcome should be. They will be standing inconspicuously on the sidelines as part of the observers.

Set up the area for a tug-of-war. Use a long rope with knots tied along each end so people can get a better grip as they pull. Mark a center line.

Instruct a group of 10-14 players. They have to decide which group they want to be on. Let them hear the urging going on in the background from each side. The three negative coaches say things like, "Those guys are wimps, we can easily beat them. Anyone who wants to help us, gets candy!" (Show inexpensive pieces of candy the players get if they choose their side.)

The three positive coaches try to entice them to be on their team by telling them, "We can win if we work together! We're strong, we'll use everything we have to win. I know this is the team you want to be on. Come and join your friends!"

The ministering angels should be strong, older boys or men standing on each side line. Remember, the participants should not know these people have a part in the game. They'll just be standing there like part of the cheering section.

After the players have chosen sides, start the tug-of-war. There will probably be more people on the negative side than the positive side. If it looks as though the positive side is losing, the ministering angels will step in one by one and pull for that side to make sure the positive side wins.

After the game, gather the group together and remind them that if they're doing what they should be doing, they will always come out ahead. Heavenly Father will send in his helpers, just as these helpers were sent in, when they're needed. Give the winning team a reward like miniature candy bars. Something bigger than the negative team got when choosing their team. The negative side gets no additional reward—they've had their temporary gratification. Sometimes in the confusion it's hard to see which team you should be on.

How To Turn Being Square Into Stepping Stones Out of cardboard, cut out 18-1 foot squares and 10-1 foot circles. Designate a start and finish line about fifty feet apart.

Divide the group as follows, giving them the instructions needed for their team.

Team 1— 8 girls This team is given nine squares, one for each person plus one extra square. The object of this team is to get to the finish line. The team members can only step on the squares. They do this by passing the extra square from the back of the line up to the front where it's placed on the floor so they can take another step. This leaves the extra square at the back of the line again. It keeps being passed to the front as they take a step. This continues until they reach the finish line.

Team 2— 1 girl This team is given nine squares. She too can only walk on the squares. She will lay the squares down in a line, walk to the back and pick up the last square, take it to the front, then go back to the back for the next square, again taking it to the front. This continues until she reaches the finish line.

Opposition— 5 girls Each girl on this team is given two circles. She can go wherever she wants as long as she is stepping on her circles. She moves by stepping on one circle, picking up the one not being used and putting it in front of her, stepping on that one while she picks up the other circle. This team's object is not to reach the finish line but to hinder the progress of the other teams. She can weave in and out, placing her circles on the other teams' squares, but EACH GIRL MUST KEEP MOVING!
Any extra girls can cheer the teams on from the sidelines.

When the game is over, bring the group together and discuss what happened in the game such as: Team 1 worked together and gave each other support. Team 2 was all alone but kept working toward her goal. The girls with circles slowed the others down but couldn't stop them. The girl working alone progressed more slowly then the other. Remember to turn peer pressure to your benefit—support your friends and work together.

KNOWLEDGE

FLIGHT THROUGH LIFE

We need to learn about careers and occupations in order to make the choices we need in this life.
With increased knowledge, our "flight through life" will be smoother.

Activity Introduction:

To present the activity you will need to bring:

1 clear glass mixing bowl

1 clear cup of sugar

1 bag of regular marshmallows

1 bag of miniature marshmallows

The marshmallows will represent the large and small amounts of knowledge we have gained through life and the sugar represents spirituality.

(Place bowl on the table.) Talk about knowledge and the fact we have been learning since the day we were born. We learned to balance so we could walk. (drop 1 marshmallow in the bowl) We learned sounds so we could talk. (drop 1 marshmallow in the bowl) We learned to count. (drop in another marshmallow) Continue dropping a marshmallow each time you name something we've learned, until the bowl is full of large and small marshmallows. Point out that the bowl seems to be full so we must have enough knowledge. But remember, no matter how much knowledge we obtain here on earth, there's always room for spirituality. (Pour the sugar over the marshmallows.)

Give each girl a handout and invite her to attend the seminar on careers.

Handout:

Copy on white card stock.

"Man's flight through life is sustained by the power of his knowledge."
Hugh B. Brown

Activity:

Give each girl a "Flight Through Life" pin and let her sign her name on the card. The remainder of the time will be spent in the seminars.

Preparation:

Copy a Flight Through Life card for each girl. Purchase an inexpensive pin with wings at a craft or novelty store to pin to the top of the card.

Two weeks before the activity, invite four people who have successful careers to come and talk to the girls for 15 minutes about their chosen professions. Some things that could be covered are: why they chose this particular career, what education they needed or what interesting things happened to them while pursuing their education and career. It would be interesting if they brought something to show the girls that's related to their field.

Some career ideas are: teachers,airline workers, mothers, artists, and people in the medical,real estate, law enforcement, or computer field.

Flight Through Life Pin

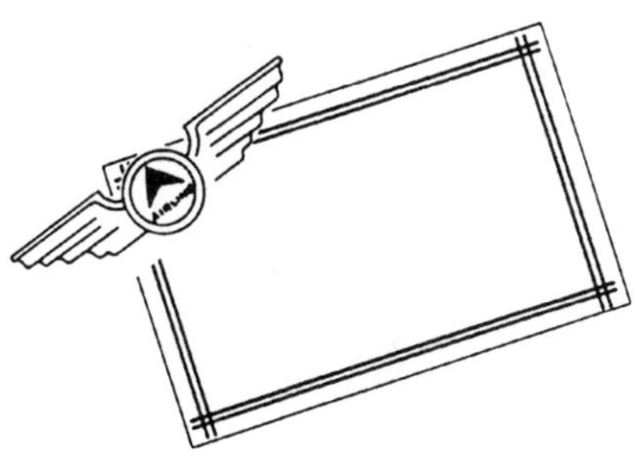

LOVE ONE ANOTHER

The word "love" has many meanings. In this activity the meaning of "love one another" is emphasized.

Activity Introduction:

To present the activity you will need to bring:

A plastic glass

A goblet made of thin glass

Fill both glasses half full of water. Heavy goblets made of thick glass do not work well. Practice at home making your goblet sing. The glass needs to be thin so it will vibrate and make a clear tone. Fill the goblet half full of water and hold on to the base to keep it steady. Do not hold the stem or bowl or it will not vibrate. Using your other hand, dip the first two fingers in the water and rub it quickly along the rim of the goblet. Continue to circle the rim quickly until you hear the singing note.

Every goblet is different so it may take a few minutes for you to make it work. Here are some hints to help. 1. Press very hard as you circle the rim and slowly release the pressure. 2. Circle the rim very fast and then slow down until you find the right speed. 3. Tilt your hand so that even though your two fingers are held together only one of them touches the glass.

Show the two glasses. Liken our lives to the plastic glass or the goblet and your fingers to love. If our life is cloudy and thick like this plastic glass and we add love, nothing happens. (Dip your fingers in the water and circle the rim of the plastic glass.) If we make our life clear and beautiful like this goblet, when we add love, (Dip your fingers in the water and circle the rim of the goblet.) It will make our whole being sing!

Handout:

For each girl make a copy of the tag. Tie it on the stem of a carnation with a ribbon.

Love is like a flower.
Each blossom does its part.
Every petal is perfection,
That really warms your heart.

Activity:

Introduce the speaker.

After the speaker the girls should have warm feelings for each other. Move the chairs in a large circle. Pass out a paper and pencil to each girl. It doesn't matter which girl's name is on the top. Pass the papers to the right and receive them from the left. As the girls receive a paper she writes a sentence or two about a quality they like about the person listed on the paper. When she receives the paper with her name on it, she will write something good about herself. Continue until the papers have completed the circle. At the end of the activity make sure each girl gets her own list and a flower with the poem.

End the activity with the song, "Love One Another".

Preparation:

Assign a group of girls to sing Love One Another.

Invite an enthusiastic youth speaker to give a short talk about loving one another, or you may want to ask one of the girls to tell about a time in her life when love really made a difference.

Write each girl's name on the top of a blank piece of paper.

Bring a pencil for each girl.

Copy a tag for each handout.

Buy a carnation for each girl and tie the tag on for the handout.

MISSIONARY SURVIVAL WEEK END

We are often told that we are each a missionary.
This activity is an enjoyable way to show the girls some of the preparation needed to become a missionary.

Activity Introduction:

To present the activity you will need to bring:

1 bowl with a "potential members" sign on it
1/2 pint of ice cold unwhipped cream
Electric beater or an egg beater.

Pour the cream in the bowl. (Be sure the bowl is cold or the cream won't whip very well.) If we want to become good missionaries we need to work efficiently with our Heavenly Father. Just as these beaters are timed to move together, we too have to move in time. (Turn the beater on.) Even if we are working together smoothly, if all we are doing is stirring up the air, nothing is being accomplished. (Turn the beaters off.) However, if we apply ourselves to someone who is ready to hear the gospel, (put the beaters in the whipped cream and turn it on.) then we can all see the results. The harder we work (turn the beaters on high) the faster we see results.

Handout:

Copy and give one to each girl.

Our life is but a mission,
A time of hope and dreams.
There's not time enough to do it all.
We have to choose, it seems.

So, while we try to do what's right,
And what's important, too.
Remember to share your testimony,
Something only you can do.

Activity:

We all know that we are supposed to be examples and live our lives so we are missionaries every day. Our lives should represent our testimonies. But some of us will be called as full time missionaries. Let's do a few things this week end to see if we will be ready for this time in our lives.

For the activity they will be assigned to be in groups of two. They will stay with their assigned companion until the end of the activity. Arise and meet at 6:30 a.m. and have individual prayers. Eat breakfast. (If possible have each pair make their own breakfast.) Set aside the time from 7:00 to 7:30 a.m. for scripture study for each set of companions.

Meet together as a group for song, prayer, and a short talk to set the proper tone. Divide into groups and rotate every 10 minutes from class to class.

Meet together again to share testimonies and close with prayer.

Preparation:

Find a house large enough for the group and divide them in groups of two. Use this for your "Missionary Training Center".

Buy items needed for breakfast.

Invite a returned missionary or a priesthood leader to give a short talk on preparing for a mission.

Ask five adults to each be in charge of a 10 minute mini-class. Some suggestions for the classes are:

1. How to prepare a simple meal.
2. How to iron a shirt well.
3. How to remove spots and press a suit.
4. How to sort clothes for washing and other washing hints.
5. How to sew on buttons in the right place.

September 2002

HYMN & HER PIT STOP

This is a different way to become more familiar with some of our church songs. The girls will love it!

Activity Introduction:

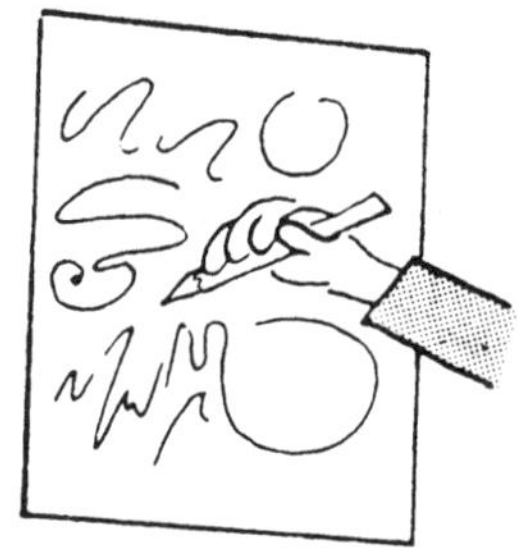

To present the activity you will need to bring:

A cassette with about six to eight minutes of all different types of music recorded on it. (Just a few lines from each song.)
A cassette player
A large piece of paper and pencil for each girl

Pass out the paper and pencils. As they play, they need to listen carefully to the different kinds of music and draw lines, circles, swirls, etc. to the way the music affects them. After this is done, ask them how the different kinds of music made them feel. If music can have that big of an effect on how we feel, we need to be very careful of the kind of music we listen to.

Give them an invitation to the "Hymn & Her Pit Stop".

Invitation:

Fill in the information and copy the invitation.

Join our "Hymn & Her Pit Stop"

Date:
Time:
Place:

We will meet at ______________________.

You will ride with ______________________.

You must have a signed permission slip from your parent or guardian to attend this activity.

Activity:

Give each group their car assignment, instruction page, and their bag. Remind them that if they are going to win, they all have to participate with enthusiasm and everything they need is in the bag.

As the cars return, look for evidence that they have each completed their "Hymn & Her Pit Stop."

Preparation:

Get permission in advance for this activity. You will need an adult driver for each car.

Divide the young women in groups of 4-5, with an adult driver in charge. Assign each car a number to help keep track of everyone.

Make a list for each group, changing the order so everyone is not trying to do the same thing at once.

Make a traveling bag for each group. In each bag put:

- A quarter
- 1 small roll of masking tape
- 1 red balloon
- 1 small American flag
- 1 small bag of crackers
- 1 safety pin
- 1 tin can and string
- A paperback copy of The Book of Mormon
- A pencil
- A large scrap of paper
- A pair of scissors

Take cookies or other treats to the Bishop. These can be handed out as each group comes by and sings.

Hymn & Her Pit Stop

Do not tape anything to the windows that will obscure the driver's vision.

1. Call ____________________ (leader's name) to report in. Tell her the number of your car. With all the enthusiasm you can come up with, sing your favorite hymn to her over the phone. Hang a red balloon on your car.
2. Drive to the nearest public place. Get out and hold the flag for all to see. Each person in the group will put their right hand over their heart and sing "The Star Spangled Banner." Write down your location__________________________ Tape the flag to the inside bottom right hand corner of your windshield.
3. Find the nearest public lawn to lie on. Lie on your back and gaze at the sky as you all sing "Oh What Do You Do In The Summer Time." Pick four blades of grass and tape them on your side window.
4. Go to the nearest grocery store and march outside the length of the store twice singing "Onward Christian Soldiers" while eating the crackers. Attach the empty bag to the back bumper of the car.
5. Sing "Book of Mormon Stories." Decide with tact someone you could give the Book of Mormon to. Sign it and make arrangements about who will present it to that person.
6. Go to a ward member's home of your group's choice and sing "There is Beauty All Around" at their front door. Ask that person to cut a heart out of a scrap of paper and sign it. Pin it on the driver.
7. Go to the Bishop's home and sing at his doorstep, "Shall the Youth of Zion Falter." The Bishop is expecting you and has a treat for you.
8. Go to a ward member's home of your group's choice and sing, "Count Your Many Blessings." Ask for an item to be donated to the Deseret Industries. Have someone in the group donate her sock and tie it to the door handle.
9. Encircle a tree holding hands and sing, "Popcorn Popping On an Apricot Tree." Pick a dandelion or other weed and tape it to the car window.
10. Go to the nearest park. The driver will lead the group singing "Do As I'm Doing" while doing at least five different activities. (Skipping, jumping, crawling, etc.) Tie the can to the bumper.
11. Meet back at the starting place.

NATURE WITH THE LUNCH-BUNCH

This is an excellent way to appreciate the day, sharing special time out of doors with your friends.

Activity Introduction:

To present the activity you will need to bring:

A picnic table cloth
A picnic basket
4 styrofoam ants
(Directions are below.)

Enter with the table cloth over your shoulder and the picnic basket in your hand. Without speaking, spread the table cloth and get down on your knees as if you were preparing a picnic. One by one, remove an ant displaying a sign. The first sign reads, "We don't want to eat alone." The second sign, "Come join us at our picnic." The third sign, "Date, time, and place." The last sign will tell them what to bring.

Invitation:

Fill in information and copy. Attach to styrofoam ant.

NATURE WITH THE LUNCH-BUNCH

Come and join us.
It won't be a picnic without you and the ants!

DATE:
TIME:
PLACE:
BRING:

Ant for invitation:

For each ant you will need:

2–2 inch Styrofoam balls for the body
1–1 1/2 inch Styrofoam ball for the head
2–6 inch pipe cleaners for the front legs
2–5 inch pipe cleaners for the back legs
2–3 inch pipe cleaners for the antennas
2 toothpicks
2 5/16 inch wiggly eyes
Black spray paint
Glue

Glue parts together as you go. Insert the toothpick to hold both parts of the body together. Use the other toothpick to attach the head. Shape the legs like this, inserting shorter legs in the rear. Glue on eyes and attach antennas. Make an indention for the mouth, with the edge of a dull knife. Spray black.

Activity:

A picnic is a fun way to spend part of a day. Plan this activity along with a hike or bicycle ride, depending on what facilities are available and what your group prefers.

Whether this is a bicycle ride or a hike, enjoy it as you go. Make your pace leisurely enough so you can stop and climb a few trees, look at the flowers or wade in a stream.

Preparation:

Plan this activity far enough in advance so that if you are taking a bicycle ride there are enough bicycles available and make sure the bikes are in good working order. If you're taking a long hike, proper footwear is needed.

Whether hiking or bike riding. Plan your route.

Make sure everyone brings a water canteen and lunch in their day pack.

Plan a nature Scavenger Hunt. Let them hunt for a list of things that are available in your area. Such as:

1 oak leaf
2 small black pebbles
3 pieces of bark
A flower with 4 petals, etc.

If you choose to have a Scavenger Hunt, bring a prize.

OLD FASHIONED BOX LUNCH SOCIAL

We can learn a lot about social refinement by socializing with the opposite gender.

Activity Introduction:

To present the activity you will need to bring:

A pitcher made of clear glass
A drinking glass
A small container of water

Show the empty pitcher and inquire about how much water can be poured from it. (Pour some water into the pitcher.) "Now how much water can we get out of it?" "This just shows that we cannot get anything out of an activity unless we put something into it."

Invitation:

Fill in the information. Copy the horse's head and invitation on heavy paper. Glue a candy straw on the neck of the horse so it looks like a stick horse. Tie or glue the invitation about a third of the way down the straw.

COME JOIN US FOR FUN AND GAMES.
THERE WILL BE A BOX LUNCH TO SHARE.

WE'LL PLAY GAMES AND HAVE RACES.
SO PLEASE COME AND JOIN US THERE!

DATE:

TIME:

PLACE:

Activity:

Meet together for this combined activity to play games and have a "Box Lunch Social." Raffle off the lunches the girls brought to the boys. Limit for the lunch is $2.00. When the boy buys a lunch it gives him the privilege of eating with the girl that made the lunch. The boys won't know which girl brought which lunch, so it should be fun to see who has the pleasure of eating together. Even if one is 12 and the other is 16, they should find something in common with each other long enough to eat a meal. After all, this just a group of youth of different ages, and being able to converse with someone of a different age is part of being socially refined.

Preparation:

Ask each girl and leader to bring a lunch big enough for two. Keep in mind the large appetite of a teenage boy. Ask them to put the lunch in a shoe box and wrap the box attractively. Each lunch will be taken at the door and assigned a number.

Set up a long table to put the box lunches on to display, before raffling them off.

Set up an eating area. This can be tables and chairs, or blankets on the floor.

Plan plenty of simple games to play before and after eating. Below are a few suggestions.

Hand each girl and her lunch partner a puzzle and pencil with their lunch. The puzzle must be filled out together after they finish eating. A prize could be given.

Fill in the the first or last name of someone starting with the letter.

S ______________________
H ______________________
A ______________________
R ______________________
E ______________________

A ______________________

L ______________________
U ______________________
N ______________________
C ______________________
H ______________________

Game Suggestions

Three-legged race

Marbles

Bobbin' for apples

Gunnysack race

Doughnuts on a string Tie 10 doughnuts on a 15 foot heavy string. Pull the string taut neck high to the contestants The 10 participants keep their hands behind their back. They are given two minutes to eat the doughnut. The first person to eat the doughnut wins. Hang 10 more doughnuts and start a new group.

Licorice eating contest Each couple gets one strand of lace licorice. They both put one end of the licorice in their mouth. When the leader says "Go!" they chew as fast as they can and see which couple can eat their licorice first.

RED, WHITE, AND YOU!

Patriotism is a lot like spiritualism. If we don't stop and concentrate on it from time to time, we might lose it.

Activity Introduction:

To present the activity you will need to:

Bring an invitation for each girl

Assign a girl's group to sing "This Land is Your Land"

Invite the girls group to sing. After the musical pressentation, hand out the invitations to the "Red, White, and You" flag ceremony.

Invitation:

Fill in the information and copy on heavy white paper. Color red, white, and blue. Cut out Uncle Sam and the invitation. Also cut around the beard and fingers so the hands can hold the card. Glue to the front of Uncle Sam as shown with the fingers curled around the front of the card..

Please join our flag ceremony
Red, White, & You!

Date:

Time:

Place:

HAPPY BIRTHDAY USA!

Handout:

A small American flag or a small American flag pin for each girl.

Activity:

For a special feeling on patriotism, meet at the flag pole early in the morning just as the sun rises. As the girls assemble, play patriotic music quietly in the background.

Raise the flag, have opening prayer, and a song. Turn the time over to the speaker. After the speaker, sing two more songs. Pass out the flags and have closing prayer.

Preparation:

Purchase either a small American flag or a small American flag pin for each girl.

Invite someone to give a rousing 15 minute speech on patriotism.

Assign someone to lead the singing.

Bring a cassette player and patriotic tapes.

Ask a group of girls to sing "This Land Is Your Land" for the lesson help.

YOU & ME & SUGAR-FREE

This activity shows how important it is to be in control of our bodies, even if it means a little self-denial. It can be fun to use a little will power and learn to know our bodies better.

Activity Introduction:

To present the activity you will need to:

> *Assign one of the leaders to come in wearing a jogging suit, panting, puffing and complaining about being exhausted. She'll pull a candy bar out of her pocket and frantically eat it. While she eats it she will display extreme relief. After eating it she will feel remorse and comment about needing to start eating better and exercising more.*

After the jogging suit display, the leader doing the presentation passes out the invitations and encourage the girls to be aware of what they're eating between now and the activity. Ask everyone to refrain from eating sugar for 48 hours before the activity.

Invitation:

For each invitation you will need an individual packet of sugar or a sugar cube wrapped in foil. Fill in the information and copy the invitation. With a piece of yarn, tie the invitation on the sugar.

You & Me & Sugar Free

Can you stay away from sugar?
Do you think you really can?

No more sweets for 48 hours.
Boy, you'll really have to plan.

Watch what you eat and try real hard.
We know you'll do your best

We'll meet with you next week,
To see who has passed the test.

Date:

Time:

Place:

Handout:

Print the award on card stock. Write in the girl's name and let each girl's leader sign her award.

You & Me & Sugar-free Award

Presented to ________________________ **for refraining from eating sugar for 48 hours.**

Sugar is great in its time and place.
But I won't let it get it's hold on me.
It's me who chooses what I'll eat.
And on this I'm sure you'll agree.

For 48 hours I ignored you, sugar.
And it really wasn't so bad.
I ate very nutritiously,
And now I'm ever so glad!

The Sugar-fiend

____

Leader' signature

Activity:

Meet together for a 10 minute lesson. Follow this by handing out the awards to the girls and leaders that refrained from eating sugar for 24 hours. Share an hour of "Jazzercise". Serve refreshments and pin a "Fruit of Physical Fitness" on the girls.

Preparation:

Invite someone to give a ten minute class on nutrition and bring a nutrition chart.

Bring a cassette player and a jazzercize tape the girls would enjoy.

Prepare trays of cut up fruit, vegetables, and dip for refreshments.

Copy the "Fruits of Physical Fitness," color, and cut out.

Fruit of Physical Fitness

So glad you "turnip-ed"

Your shape is so "a-peeling"

You got "plum" tuckered out.

The most enthusiastic "Pear".

You "squashed" out fatigue.

The most enthusiastic "Pear".

April 2000

SERVICE SCAVENGER HUNT

When service is performed correctly, it can almost seem like a game.
For this activity, we are going to change serving into a game.

Activity Introduction:

To present the activity you will need to bring:

1 small cake
(If you group is small, you may want to bring enough cake to serve everyone after the demonstration.)
A small decorative plate
1 fork
2 napkins
Cake server

Ask who would like to have a piece of cake. Choose two volunteers. Serve the first girl properly with the cake server. Place her cake on the decorative plate and hand her the cake, a fork and a napkin. Serve the second girl by taking a piece of cake roughly in your hand, plop it on a napkin and hand it to her. Ask if they noticed the difference in the way you served the two girls. How did the two girls feel?

Our lives will not be well-rounded until we take time to serve. Sometimes we get so busy doing everyday things, that before we realize it we have not done anything for anyone else. There are two ways to serve. Just as the cake was served, we can do it graciously with love or we can do it halfheartedly and just go through the motions. It's not just that you serve others, but how you serve them!

Give the girls an invitation to the "Service Scavenger Hunt."

Invitation:

Copy an invitation for each girl.

Please join us for our Service Scavenger Hunt

Don't forget to take time to serve others,
In whatever way you can.
We've always been told to do this,
Ever since time began.

It not only benefits us,
It benefits others, too.
We can always spread a little pleasure,
With the things we choose to do!

Date:

Time:

Place:

Activity:

Divide into teams of [illegible]s and give them a pencil and a list of service jobs they need to do. The teams will have 45 minutes [illegible]mplete the Service Scavenger Hunt. Make sure that one girl in each group has a watch. They must ret[illegible]n 45 minutes. Give them points if they complete everything on the list and return early. Deduct points for each minute the team is late. They receive the allotted points for each thing they completed on their list. The girls on each team will stay together going from house to house. When they return, total up the points and give a prize for the team with the most points. Serve refreshments.

Preparation:

For safety, do this activity in an area you know well.

Assign someone on each team to bring a hand vacuum, window cleaner, needle and thread, and anything else you feel they need to provide for the scavenger hunt.

Copy a scavenger list

Bring a pencil for each group.

Get a funny prize for the winning team.

Plan and prepare refreshments.

Service Scavenger Hunt

Make a check mark for each item completed.

( ) Fold four towels. *1 point*
( ) Wash one window. *4 points*
( ) Roll up one garden hose. *3 points*
( ) Feed the cat. *2 points*
( ) Bring in someone's newspaper. *2 points*
( ) Sew on a button. *4 points*
( ) Play "Ring Around the Rosy" with a willing child. *4 points*
( ) Pull ten weeds. *3 points*
( ) Sweep off a porch. *3 points*
( ) Pick up five pieces of litter. *3 points*
( ) Dust two end tables. *2 points*
( ) Sit and visit for three minutes with an adult. *5 points*
( ) Pick up twenty baby toys. *5 points*
( ) Bring in someone's mail. *1 point*
( ) Vacuum a front room. *4 points*
( ) Read a short story to a child. *5 points*

FEAST OR FAMINE

We can find more spiritual things in our lives if we are spiritually aware of our surroundings. It's difficult to be sensitive to these feelings, unless we try to focus our thoughts and feelings in a spiritual direction.

Activity Introduction:

To present the activity you will need to bring:

An elegant table setting for one

A worn out, tarnished table setting for one

Use your imagination to describe serving a delicious meal on the delicate dinnerware. You may serve a slice of tender roast beef cooked to perfection, hot vegetables with a pat of butter, smooth creamy mashed potatoes topped with pools of creamy well-seasoned gravy. Ask, "If you weren't hungry before, are you getting hungry now? Can you see images of scrumptious food in your mind? Have I whet your appetite for food?"

Show the worn out, tarnished table setting. Pretend you no longer have delicious food. You're often hungry and are lucky if some days you sit down to one meager meal a day. If this one meager meal is all that is available to you, do you think you would be just as hungry for your meager meal as another person who often dines in elegance is hungry for their meal?

Our spiritual appetites can be compared to this. Sometimes we feast elegantly on spirituality and other times we find ourselves starving spiritually because we feed ourselves such a meager spiritual meal.

Invite the girls to attend the "Feast or Famine" activity.

Activity:

Give the girls a handout and ask them what they can see in the picture. (Their response will be flowers, grass, etc.) Tell them you are going to help them see more clearly by sharing your testimony with them. Bear your testimony and end by acknowledging the fact that Heavenly Father will teach us if we seek his guidance. Inform them that you have a "Testimony Magnifying Glass." Ask them to look at their handouts through the glass and see if they can find something in there that Heavenly Father would want them to know.

After the girls have looked through the glass, someone will comment that what Heavenly Father would want them to know is written in the flower. (In the largest flower on the right you will find the message, "My daily actions will reflect my Spiritual Awareness." After you have used the glass to bring the message to their attention, you can now easily see it without the magnifying glass. That is because you are now aware of what you are looking for. As we look for guidance and help from our Father in Heaven, our alertness will grow and we will find our awareness multiplied.

After the speaker, serve light refreshments.

Preparation:

Invite a speaker to talk to the youth on "Feast or Famine—Spiritual Awareness."

Prepare and bring the handouts.

Bring a large magnifying glass.

Plan and prepare refreshments.

Handout:

Copy on card stock.

FOR ALL ETERNITY

Marriage is an important step and we shouldn't take lightly.
If marriage takes place in the right location, (the temple) and for the right reasons, then marriage is the right step.

Activity Introduction:

To present the activity you will need to bring:

1 engagement ring

(Hold up the engagement ringfor everyone to see.) Talk about the ring and what it symbolizes. Some of the things mentioned might be a deep love, commitment to each other, etc. Make the observation that the ring is round, having no beginning or ending. This also symbolizes eternity.

Handout:

For each handout you will need:

A new spool of white thread
A copy of the tag
Narrow ribbon to tie the tag on

Copy the tag and punch a small hole in the corner. Insert the ribbon and tie the tag to the spool of thread.

My Special Spool of Thread

This white spool of thread has a very special meaning. White stands for purity and cleanliness in word, thought, and deed. It is also a sacred color that is worn within the House of the Lord. This thread can be used to make my wedding dress which I'll wear to the Temple. I will strive to keep my life as clean and pure as white on this spool of thread. To do this, I will follow the council of my Father in Heaven and obey His commandments. All of these things I will do, not only to prepare myself to enter the Temple, but to remain worthy to return back to the presence of my Heavenly Father.

Preparation:

Ask people to take part in the skit. You will need someone to play the part of:

Bishop, Jim Hansen	Mother	Future husband	Small girl
Julia Harriett	Father	Class advisor	Neighbor

Invite a group to sing the songs in the skit.

Pre-record the thoughts on cassette of the Bishop, Julia, her father, her mother, her neighbor, and her advisor.

For stage props you will need:
Spot light, quiet music (including the Wedding March), tape recorder, 8 chairs, wedding decorations

Activity:

Temple Marriage Skit

JULIA: *Preparing for bed and starting to dream.* I wonder if I'm dating the right kind of boys? Jim is so much fun to be with. I wonder if he's the one for me? *The bed is removed from the stage as the other scenes appear.*

The dream scene opens with wedding decorations displayed. Four chairs on the right and four chairs on the left of the stage. Prelude music is played until the Bishop takes center stage. Spot light is on him.

BISHOP: The bride and groom have asked me, Bishop _____________ to extend to you their thanks for coming to witness their wedding ceremony this day. *He looks around and the cassette starts playing as if he's thinking out loud.*

BISHOP TAPE: Jim Hansen and Julia Harriet. How fast they have both grown. (Music starts) It seems as though it was only yesterday that Jim received his first merit badge and Julie graduated from Primary. I can remember when they first started dating. From the stand I noticed Julia watching Jim. Then he would turn to watch her. She would quickly avoid his eyes so he wouldn't suspect she'd been looking. Jim didn't come to church there for quite a while. I was a little concerned about that. I was happy when Julie started encouraging him to come to church with her. I really should have been more concerned about them dating when it was evident that Jim's attitude toward the church wasn't good. I didn't realize that it had gotten serious so quickly. I wish Jim would have considered going on a mission, but he didn't get much encouragement along that line.

Julie, I remember your last interview with me before you left the Young Women's program. You told me that someday you wanted a special home just like the one your parents raised you in. Your eyes sparkled when you talked of someday finding an eternal companion, one who had the same goals as you, who would take you to the Temple of the Lord. You wanted someone who would honor his priesthood and lead you and your future family in prayer, scripture reading, and family home evening.

I tried then to discourage you from dating someone who might never have the same eternal goals as you, just to lessen the chance of falling in love. You assured me that dating Jim was just "fun" . You said it wasn't serious and you certainly didn't intend to marry him. Now you are about to enter into a marriage where the contract between you and your chosen companion will endure only until "death do you part." Why have you made this decision? Have you considered how you are putting your eternal goals in jeopardy? Are you sure you're ready to risk losing so much? TAPE OFF, SPOT LIGHT OFF, MUSIC OFF.

JIM: *Enters the stage and shakes hands with the Bishop.* MUSIC ON
Whew… I can't wait to get out of this monkey suit. Just look at all these people! I guess I should be used to crowds, but somehow it's different when you're playing on the basketball court. I'm sure lucky to be marrying a girl like Julia. She's one special girl and I really do love her. I'll be glad when today's over though. Then she'll be mine and I won't have to waste time going to church every Sunday. Don't take me wrong, Bishop. Going to church is all right if you don't have anything important to do. If I'm going to make it in professional basketball, I have to concentrate on my career. Once I'm at the top,

I'll be able to afford all the important things I'd like to give Julia. Boy I'm hot! *He wipes his brow.* I sure wish she'd hurry! MUSIC & SPOT LIGHT OFF.

JULIA: *Julie comes up the aisle on her father's arm . Her mother, Advisor, and neighbor come in and are seated on chairs. She looks as though she's thinking.* JULIA TAPE ON My wedding day, I can hardly believe it's here! If anyone would have told me I was getting married before I was nineteen, I would have laughed at them. But, what's a girl supposed to do when she falls in love, especially when that someone is a special person like Jim. Doesn't he look handsome in that suit? *Pause* I'm so happy, I wish today could last forever. I hope Mom and Dad aren't too disappointed that we aren't marrying in the temple. I know that after we're married, I can persuade Jim to go with me to be sealed in the temple. We love each other so much that surely nothing could possibly get in the way. If they knew Jim the way I do, they wouldn't be worried. *Pause* There's the Bishop. I can't help thinking of the terrific talk we had at my last interview. *Pause* I hope I've made the right decision! I guess I'm suffering from last minute jitters. TAPE, MUSIC, AND SPOT LIGHT OFF

Julia is standing by Jim and her father goes and sits by her mother.

BISHOP: Brothers and Sisters, we meet today to join Jim Hansen and Julia Harriett in marriage. I am glad they have asked me, their Bishop, to marry them.

The Lord planned that men and women would find each other and have a happy family relationship. In the scriptures he said," Therefore, shall a son leave his father and his mother and shall cleave unto his wife; and they shall be one flesh." As you say your vows today you will be forming a partnership with each other. Now is the time for you to plan a good strong marriage and organize and set your goals so your marriage which will be beautiful and rewarding. Now, if there is no one here who objects, let us proceed with the ceremony.

FATHER: *He looks as though he's thinking.* SPOTLIGHT, MUSIC, AND TAPE ON
Oh Julia, my dear, sweet daughter. I wish I could object. So many times I have tried to take from my own heart the feelings I have about the temple and graft them into your heart. I remember looking at temple pictures with you and driving past the temple and saying, "This is where your mother and I were married."

I remember that special family home evening we had when you were younger. I asked if I could tell you about your future. You said, "Yes" and I said something like, "Julia when you get older, you'll meet a young man and you'll come home to me and say 'Dad, I met a boy I really like a lot.' Then I'll meet him and I'll like him too. Then one day you'll come home and say, "Dad, I don't just like him, I love him, and I want to marry him!" And I'd give you my blessings." Very early in the morning on that special day I'll come to your room and touch your shoulder and whisper, "Julia, it's time to get up, it's your wedding day." Then we'd drive through the morning air and park as close as we can to the temple.

Once inside we'll all dress in white and go to a room where people get married forever. I'll look at you and think you're the most beautiful daughter in the world—but you won't be looking at me, you'll be looking at him. The room will be peaceful and beautiful. A man of God will be there, one who is ordained to perform that sacred covenant and he will talk to you about your marriage. He'll ask you and your chosen mate to kneel, one on each side of a beautiful alter. As you kneel your hands will join in an eternal clasp. Your wedding ceremony will be performed through the Priesthood of God. On that day a partnership will be formed between you, your companion and your Heavenly Father. That partnership will last forever.

Oh Julia, how different this marriage is from the one we talked about that night. A man of God is here and he will perform your wedding ceremony, but when he is finished you'll only be married until this life is over. The story of your union will end. Just as your marriage to Jim will come to an end. My dear sweet Julia, how hard your mother and I have tried to teach you, to show you through our example, how important a celestial marriage is. But the decision is yours. It has to be. How my heart aches. Do you know how much I love you? TAPE, MUSIC, AND SPOT LIGHT OFF.

MOTHER: *He looks as though he's thinking.* SPOT LIGHT ON MOTHER AND TAPE STARTS.
Object? Oh Julia, you are my daughter, so precious and dear to me. I love you so much. This is your wedding day, one of the most important days of your life. The decorations are lovely. You look so beautiful in your dress, and your friends and family are here. The whole atmosphere is exciting and sweet, but Julia, if you just knew what you are missing. MUSIC STARTS

The day your father and I went to the temple to be married for time and eternity was one of the most glorious days of our lives. A day we will cherish and hold dear forever. I recall that your grandmother, my mother, slipped a piece of paper under my pillow the night before my wedding. It said, "Enter the temple as if the floor within were made of gold; and every wall of jewels; all of wealth untold. As if a choir in robes of fire were singing there. No shout, no rush, only hush ... for God is here."

Julia, from the moment we entered that holy building, the feelings of peace was overpowering. Never before had we felt so united with each other and our Heavenly Father. That glorious day we pledged our eternal love and fidelity each for the other, not just before our friends and loved ones, but in the presence of God and angels. The day we were sealed was the day I really fell in love with your father. I know you sincerely love Jim, but is that enough? If only you would have held out for a temple marriage. We would have given you the support you needed. I love you, Julia. The decision is yours.

SONG: "What Do You Do When The Going Gets Rough And The Journey is Tough" (Music from Saturday's Warriors)

NEIGHBOR: *She looks as though she's thinking.* SPOT LIGHT AND TAPE ON
Julia, even though I'm only your friend and neighbor, I would give anything if I could object to this wedding. MUSIC STARTS I have watched as you have grown to a very special young woman. It makes me sad when I see you make the same mistake I did when I got married. I, like you, grew up in a strong L.D.S. family like yours. But I wasn't committed to temple marriage. I fell in love with a man much like Jim. I kept telling myself he would change his attitude toward the church once we were married. We had our first baby, Ben. Time went by, some things were better some things got worse. But we didn't always feel like a close family. Sometimes I felt we were just three people living together under one roof. Over the years more babies came, but the arguments over the time spent on church things has not stopped. There is great anxiety in not knowing how it will be when we come home from a church meeting. Will it be silence chilled with words not spoken, or a raise of the eyebrows that dismisses the entire subject. Our sweet children can feel the anger, the heartache and the bitterness. Often they cry because they know things are not as they should be. I love Ben, but my heart aches over the years that have passed because he has not seen fit to take us to the temple. How frightening. How final. How devastating to realize that my marriage, my children, and my family life will end with death, because I failed to follow God's instructions. I wish I had been more committed to all the blessings and promises of a temple marriage. I hope and pray that things will work out better for you. TAPE, MUSIC, AND SPOT LIGHT OFF.

LAUREL ADVISOR: *She looks as though she's thinking.* SPOT LIGHT AND TAPE ON.
My mind has been busy playing back bits and pieces of the lessons I gave you when you were in my class. I too, have a great concern for your future happiness. MUSIC STARTS Julia, do you remember who you are? You are a daughter of God and because you are His daughter, you have the potential to receive all the glories and blessings that God has promised His children. You are entitled to queendom. You are heir to the great fortunes of eternal life. What will you do with this prized inheritance? The Lord is very specific and very definite on what he requires of each of us, Julia. The temple endowment is one of the ordinances that is required to enable us to walk back to the presence of our Father in Heaven. Without this endowment we will not be allowed to pass by the angels. You are placing your inheritance in jeopardy, all because a decision was not made and the commitment was not there. TAPE, MUSIC, AND SPOT LIGHT OFF.

SONG: "Line Upon Line, Precept Upon Precept" (Music from Saturday's Warriors)

CHILD: *Dressed in white.* SPOTLIGHT *Shine on the child as she walks down the aisle. He or she is thinking.*
I wish I were there to object. MUSIC STARTS A few short years in the future you will be my mother. Your decision to get married in the temple or not affects me too. I am with Heavenly Father now, but one day you will bring my spirit from heaven to live in our home. Julia, will I be born under the covenant? Will you teach me and prepare me to return to my Heavenly Father? Will I know the joy and happiness of belonging to an eternal family? I cannot make these decisions for myself for I am not yet born. You are making them for me, for someday you will be my mother.

SONG: "I Am a Child of God" *Child turns and goes down the aisle.* TAPE, MUSIC, AND SPOT LIGHT OFF.

MUSIC STARTS AS SPOT LIGHT PICKS UP FUTURE HUSBAND COMING DOWN THE AISLE.

TEMPLE MARRIAGE

FUTURE HUSBAND: *He's thinking.*
Julia, if you would only wait. MUSIC STARTS In a few short months, I will return from my mission and you and I will meet. If you will wait, the time will come when you will go to your dad and tell him you have met a boy you really like a lot. Then he'll meet me and he'll like me too. Our friendship will blossom and one night I will tell you that I love you and you will know that you love me too. I will ask you to be my companion, Julia, on this earth and forever as we continue into eternity. On the appointed day you and I will enter the temple of the Lord. We'll dress in white and after you have received your endowments we'll go to the room where we'll be married forever. It will be so peaceful and beautiful there. A man of God will be there and he will talk to us about marriage. He'll ask you to kneel on one side of the altar and me on the other side. We'll hold hands and I will look at you and know you are the loveliest young woman in the world. We'll promise to be true to our Father in Heaven and to each other as husband and wife. By the power of the holy priesthood we will be sealed and a partnership will be formed that will bridge death and take us into eternity. When children bless our home we will teach them to walk in the way of the Lord and they will be ours forever. Our home will be blessed with the Priesthood. We will have prayer, scriptures, and family home evening in our home. We may or may not become rich in this life, but together we will work toward the riches of eternity. Our circle of love will grow and extend beyond days and years, for in God's eternal plan, life goes on forever and ever. Julia,. Julia, will you please wait for me? MUSIC, AND SPOT LIGHT OFF.

JULIA: *Waking up in bed looking around and stretching.* It isn't true. I'm not really getting married yet. What a wonderful but frightful dream! This dream made me realize that my choice of a husband affects so many more people than myself. No wonder the leaders have cautioned us to be prayerful in our dating.

Bright Impressions Inc.

Ideas and illustrations that motivate !

#89505	Young Women UMPH! Book Vol. 1
#89505	Young Women Vol. 1
#28809	Young Women Vol .2
#68912	Young Women Vol. 3
#19535	Girls Camp Ideas Vol. 1
#79640	Seminary Devotionals
#99018	Missionary Mailers Vol. 1
#89434	Missionary Mailers Vol. 2
#18807	Book of Mormon Companion
#48911	Family Home Evening Vol. 1
#89017	Family Home Evening Vol .2
#19431	Family Home Evening Vol. 3
#69120	Primary Activity Days Vol. 1
#49639	Primary Activity Days Vol. 2
#69329	Achievement Days Vol. 1
#59536	Achievement Days Vol. 2
#11864	Sharing Time Vol. 1
#78706	Sharing Time Vol .2
#39015	Sharing Time Vol. 3
#69016	Nursery Ideas Vol. 1
#19326	Nursery Ideas Vol .2
#18910	Homemaking Nights Vol. 1
#19119	Homemaking Nights Vol .2
#18808	Leadership Themes Vol. 1
#59328	Leadership Themes Vol .2
#78302	Invites & Handouts Vol. 2
#48603	Invites & Handouts Vol. 3

Under Construction

#99501	**Creative**Clip Bundles of Bytes CD (Over 1400 pictures! Works on both PC & Mac!)
#39423	Clip Art Gift Tags
#79537	Clip Art Critters
#89538	Clip Art Seasons & Celebrations
#69222	Pattern Prints Vol. 1
#89330	Pattern Prints Vol .2
#89121	Small Gifts Vol. 1
#39327	Small Gifts Vol .2
#89224	Scout Games Vol .2
#88913	Parties & Activities Vol. 1
#59433	Parties & Activities Vol .2
#69223	Family Reunions Vol. 1
#99225	Busy Family Cookbook (Includes one year menu, shoppling lists, recipes, substitution list and more!)

PLEASE—
Look or ask for these books in your local bookstore.
If they cannot be found
call Bright Impressions!

Bright Impression Inc. 2008 Dimple Dell Rd Sandy, Utah 84092 801-571-9744 Fax 801-523-3337

7/96